FRANKLIN D. ROOSEVELT'S
PRESIDENCY

FREEDOM UNDER THE
WITH
JUSTICE AND SEC
FOR
ALL MANKIN

FRANKLIN D. ROOS

PRESIDENTIAL POWERHOUSES

FRANKLIN D. ROOSEVELT'S

PRESIDENCY

LINDA CROTTA BRENNAN

LERNER PUBLICATIONS ◆ MINNEAPOLIS

Lerner Publications Company
A division of Lerner Publishing Group, Inc.
241 First Avenue North
Minneapolis, MN 55401 USA

For reading levels and more information, look up this title at
www.lernerbooks.com.

Main body text set in Caecilia LT Std 9.5/15.
Typeface provided by Adobe Systems.

Library of Congress Cataloging-in-Publication Data

Brennan, Linda Crotta.
    Franklin D. Roosevelt's presidency / by Linda Crotta Brennan.
        pages cm. — (Presidential powerhouses)
    ISBN 978-1-4677-7928-9 (lb : alk. paper)
    ISBN 978-1-4677-8549-5 (eb pdf)
        1. Roosevelt, Franklin D. (Franklin Delano), 1882–1945—Juvenile
literature. 2. United States—Politics and government—1933–1945—
Juvenile literature. 3. Presidents—United States—Biography—
Juvenile literature. I. Title.
E807.B746 2015
973.917092—dc23 [B]   2015000302

Manufactured in the United States of America
1 – VP – 12/31/15

★ TABLE OF CONTENTS ★

★ INTRODUCTION ★

On December 6, 1941, a young naval officer entered the White House Oval Office and handed a secret message to President Franklin Delano Roosevelt. US codebreakers had intercepted and decoded a communication sent from Japan to the Japanese ambassador in Washington, DC. The message said that the Japanese government had rejected President Roosevelt's demand that Japan give up territory it had recently seized in China and Southeast Asia. Roosevelt believed Japan's leaders would do more than simply ignore his request. Japan would likely attack the United States, pulling the country into the war that was already raging in Europe and Asia.

Harry Hopkins, the president's closest adviser, said it was a shame that the Japanese could pick their own time and place to attack the United States. Why couldn't America strike the first blow? "We can't do that," Roosevelt answered. "We are a democracy and a peaceful people."

Roosevelt knew that a preemptive strike against Japan would be hugely unpopular with the American people. The president had warned his country about the growing threat from Germany and Japan. Yet, after the horrors of World War I (1914–1918), few Americans wanted to get involved in another conflict. Many thought the broad expanses of the Atlantic and Pacific Oceans would protect the United States from the distant fighting.

The next morning, December 7, 1941, the Americans intercepted another note to the Japanese ambassador. His government instructed him to break off negotiations with the

United States at one o'clock in the afternoon. The precise timing was odd. The president thought this meant the Japanese planned to strike—perhaps at Thailand, British Malaya (present-day Malaysia), or American territory in the Philippines.

JAPAN ATTACKS

Japan had another target in mind. Roosevelt had just finished lunch when the phone in the Oval Office rang. The Navy Department had a report that the US naval base at Pearl Harbor, Hawaii, was under attack. Harry Hopkins thought it must be a mistake. The Japanese wouldn't attack Hawaii, he said. It was too far from Japan and too well defended. But the president realized the report was probably true. The Japanese had chosen to strike where they were least expected.

American sailors watch smoke rise from Hickam Field during the Japanese attack on Pearl Harbor on December 7, 1941.

At first, the president appeared calm. The Japanese had attacked American soil. This would make it easier for him to convince Congress to declare war. But throughout the chaotic afternoon, reports of American losses kept rolling in. By the end of the day, the president's face was gray and haggard. Caught totally by surprise, the US Navy had been barely able to mount a defense. More than two thousand Americans were dead, and more than one thousand wounded. Twenty ships had been sunk or damaged and more than one hundred planes had been destroyed.

MESSAGE TO THE NATION

The next day, President Franklin Delano Roosevelt was driven to the Capitol building. He rose from his wheelchair—which he'd used since contracting crippling polio at the age of thirty-nine—his

President Roosevelt addresses Congress on December 8, 1941. Following the attack on Pearl Harbor, the United States declared war with Japan.

knees locked in place by heavy steel braces. Holding the arm of his adult son James, the president walked slowly up to the speaking platform. There, he gripped the sides of the lectern to hold himself upright.

Once he was in place, only his powerful upper body was visible to the members of Congress and the visitors who packed the chamber. His strong baritone voice filled the room and was broadcast out to radio listeners across the nation: "Yesterday, December 7, 1941—a date which will live in infamy—the United States of America was suddenly and deliberately attacked by naval and air forces of the Empire of Japan." He went on, "No matter how long it may take us to overcome this premeditated invasion, the American people, in their righteous might, will win through to absolute victory."

The fate of democracy hung in the balance, yet Franklin Delano Roosevelt faced this crisis as he had faced others in his already long and eventful presidency. His irrepressible optimism and willingness to experiment with innovative government programs was pulling the country out of the Great Depression (1929–1942). He would lead the country toward victory in World War II (1939–1945) and set the course for a future of prosperity.

★ CHAPTER ONE ★

THE MAKING OF A PRESIDENT

Franklin Delano Roosevelt was born on January 30, 1882, on his family's estate overlooking the Hudson River, in Hyde Park, New York. His mother, Sara Delano Roosevelt, was descended from wealthy New England sea merchants. His father, James Roosevelt, was vice president of several corporations and lived the life of a country gentleman, managing his estate, riding its farms and fields on horseback, and socializing with other members of the upper class.

Franklin was his mother's only child. His father, who was in his fifties when Franklin was born, had been married before and widowed. Franklin had a married half-brother who was the same age as Franklin's mother.

Franklin grew up in luxury, surrounded by adults who doted on him. At Hyde Park, he accompanied his father, riding a pony across hundreds of acres of fields and forests on the estate. At his family's vacation home on Campobello Island, just north of the Canadian border, he spent his time swimming and sailing the family yacht. Ships and the sea were among Franklin's lifelong passions. Franklin's parents traveled widely, and from the time he was three, he went with them. He spent much of his childhood in Britain and elsewhere in Europe.

Franklin (left) rides on horseback with his father, James, around their home in Hyde Park, New York, in 1891. Franklin's mother, Sara, stands nearby.

SCHOOL YEARS

Tutored at home, Franklin didn't go to school until he was fourteen, when he was sent away to Groton, an exclusive prep school northwest of Boston, Massachusetts. He was initially homesick but eventually settled into his new routine. After graduating, Franklin moved to Boston and enrolled at Harvard University. Soon after, he had to rush home to see his ill father, who died on December 8, 1900. Franklin spent the holidays mourning with his mother. When Franklin returned to school in January, Sara rented an apartment in Boston so she could be closer to him.

Franklin was an active student, joining a number of clubs at Harvard. He sought membership into the most exclusive of all Harvard social clubs, the Porcellian, but was turned down. It was a major disappointment.

However, Franklin found a home at the school newspaper, the Harvard *Crimson*. As a first-year reporter, he gained a big scoop when his cousin Theodore visited campus. Theodore Roosevelt was running for vice president under William McKinley. Franklin used his cousin's visit as an opportunity to ask Harvard's president, Charles Eliot, which presidential candidate he supported. Though Eliot had previously kept his opinion a secret, Franklin managed to get an answer from him. The next day the *Crimson* ran Franklin's headline, "President Eliot declares for McKinley."

On September 4, 1901, President McKinley was shot. He died eight days later, and Theodore Roosevelt became president. During Teddy's term, Franklin attended a ball at the White House. "From start to finish it was glorious," he told his mother.

Franklin (front center) poses with classmates from the Harvard Crimson in 1904. Franklin reported on campus news and events during his time at college.

THE ROOSEVELT FAMILY

The Roosevelts were wealthy and powerful. Their roots in the United States date back to the 1640s when Claes Martenszen van Rosenvelt emigrated from the Netherlands to Manhattan, then called New Amsterdam. Claes's son changed his last name to Roosevelt. This Roosevelt became an alderman (an elected city official), beginning the family tradition of political service.

One of Claes's grandsons settled in Oyster Bay, New York. Another settled in Hyde Park, New York. US president Theodore Roosevelt and his niece, Eleanor, were members of the Oyster Bay branch of the Roosevelts. Franklin was descended from the Hyde Park Roosevelts.

Both Theodore Roosevelt (left) and his niece, Eleanor (right), were members of the Oyster Bay branch of the Roosevelt family. These photos capture Theodore at the time he became president in 1901 and Eleanor as a young woman in 1898.

ROMANCE AND MARRIAGE

Born in 1884, Eleanor Roosevelt was two years younger than Franklin, her fifth cousin once removed, and had known him when they were children. They became closer after she made her debut, or official presentation into society, in 1902. The round of formal parties and gatherings was a painful social ordeal for the shy young woman, but Franklin's attentions eased her way. Franklin was captivated by the tall, lean young woman with intelligent blue eyes. A romance developed between them.

After graduating from Harvard, Franklin entered law school at Columbia University in New York City. Franklin and Eleanor were married on March 17, 1905. President Theodore Roosevelt walked

Franklin speaks with Eleanor on the porch of his family's summer home on Campobello Island in August 1904.

his niece down the aisle and made quips about keeping the name in the family.

The couple moved into a house in New York City that Franklin's mother had bought and furnished for them. By then Eleanor was pregnant with the couple's first child, Anna, who was born in 1906. A second child, James, followed in 1907. Sara set up the growing family in a larger house, next to hers, with a connecting door between them. The couple eventually had six children, though one baby died of the flu when he was six months old.

POLITICAL BEGINNINGS

Meanwhile, Roosevelt had left Columbia without earning his degree and had passed the bar exam, qualifying him to practice law. He found a clerk's position with a prestigious New York City law firm, but the work did not suit him. He told fellow law clerks that he intended to run for political office at the first opportunity. His goal was to become president of the United States, and he mapped out a plan to reach that goal. In many respects, he would follow his cousin Teddy's path, with one main difference. Teddy was a Republican. Franklin, like his father, was a Democrat.

In 1910 Roosevelt ran for the New York State Senate. At a time when candidates still made their rounds by train or in a horse and buggy, Roosevelt hired a big, red, open-topped car and sped from town to town campaigning. He was only twenty-eight and inexperienced, but voters responded to his sincerity and charm. And as a Roosevelt, he had name recognition. Franklin was elected by a large margin.

Seasoned senators didn't think much of him at first. They called him an arrogant snob. Roosevelt made speeches about honest government, though he didn't do much to address social issues, such as child labor and substandard housing.

Roosevelt shakes hands with voters while campaigning for the New York Senate in 1910.

But Roosevelt made headlines when he took a stand against New York City's corrupt Democratic party leadership. A small group of powerful politicians known as party bosses controlled the city's elections as well as many elections for state offices. They handpicked candidates and offered voters incentives to support those candidates. The party bosses were notorious for using bribery and other illegal activities to keep Democrats in power and to make themselves rich. Shortly after taking office as a state senator, Roosevelt led a group of Democrats who refused to support the party bosses' candidate for the US Senate. In the end, Roosevelt and the bosses came to a compromise, with a candidate who was acceptable to them both.

During this time, Roosevelt gained a friend and a political mentor, Louis Howe. Originally, Howe thought Roosevelt was

a "spoiled, silk-pants sort of guy." But Howe came to admire Roosevelt's courage and would astutely guide his political career.

RISE THROUGH DEMOCRATIC PARTY RANKS

When Woodrow Wilson ran as the Democratic candidate for president in 1912, Roosevelt threw his support behind the progressive Princeton professor. After Wilson was elected, Roosevelt was offered a position as assistant secretary of the navy. Roosevelt's fascination with ships stretched back to his childhood. The offer was even more appealing because his cousin Teddy had held this position during his rise to the presidency. Roosevelt readily accepted the appointment.

Assistant Secretary Roosevelt (center) stands with members of the Brooklyn Navy Yard in front of the Army Navy Club building in Washington, DC, on December 12, 1916.

In 1914 World War I (1914–1918) broke out in Europe. Though the United States was not involved in the conflict, Roosevelt believed the US military should be ready for war. He testified before Congress, convincing lawmakers to strengthen the country's naval forces. After the United States entered World War I in 1917, Roosevelt traveled to Europe to inspect naval bases and oversaw many of his department's war-related activities.

After Roosevelt returned from one of his trips overseas, Eleanor unpacked his bags and discovered a collection of love letters. The letters had been written by Eleanor's former social secretary, Lucy Mercer. Eleanor realized that Roosevelt and Mercer were having an affair. She confronted her husband and offered him a divorce. But divorce would create a scandal and ruin Roosevelt's political career. To avoid destroying Roosevelt's presidential ambitions, the couple agreed to stay married. Roosevelt promised not to see Lucy Mercer again—a promise he would later secretly break.

In November 1918 the war ended in victory for the United States and its allies. Hoping to prevent future worldwide conflicts, President Wilson championed the creation of an international

Lucy Mercer began working for the Roosevelts in 1914. She was hired as Eleanor's social secretary and remained in the position until 1917.

peacekeeping organization called the League of Nations. While Roosevelt supported the League of Nations, he said little about it publicly. He knew that many Americans would fear that their country would have to give up too much sovereignty, or right to self-rule, if it joined the league. Wilson suffered a massive stroke in the final days of his presidency, leaving the League of Nations without a champion, and Congress refused to ratify the treaty to join the organization.

Roosevelt's rise in the Democratic Party continued. Democratic presidential candidate James M. Cox chose him for his vice president in 1920, but the pair lost the election to Republican candidate Warren Harding.

Roosevelt returned to private life, working as a lawyer while he planned his next move back into politics. He kept himself in the public eye by campaigning for others and supporting worthy causes, including the Boy Scouts. He became president of the organization's board.

DISASTER STRIKES

Roosevelt led an active life. He worked at his law office in New York City during the week, spent winter weekends at Hyde Park, and summered at Campobello. One summer weekend in 1921, he stopped at a Boy Scout camp after leaving work in New York City and then continued on to Campobello, where he spent his time sailing, swimming, and running. A few days later, Roosevelt felt chilled and his muscles ached. He went to bed early. During the night, he developed a high fever and suffered stabbing pains. His legs felt numb and lifeless.

Roosevelt was unable to walk. The family called in one doctor after another, but no one could explain what had happened. Finally, a specialist from Boston delivered the bad news. Roosevelt had polio and would remain paralyzed from the waist down.

POLIO

Roosevelt may have been exposed to polio during his visit to the Boy Scout camp. The disease is caused by a virus and is highly infectious. Most people infected with the polio virus have no symptoms or experience mild, flu-like symptoms. In a small percentage of people, polio causes paralysis and even death.

Polio attacks the nervous system, and the disease once crippled tens of thousands of Americans, mostly children, each year. In 1953 Jonas Salk developed the first vaccine to protect against it, and the United States has had very few known polio cases since 1979. The disease still occurs in a few poor and unstable countries, such as war-torn Afghanistan.

Eleanor nursed her husband around the clock. Certain that his political life was finished, Roosevelt's mother tried to convince him to retire to Hyde Park and let her watch over him. But he insisted his career wasn't over.

Roosevelt spent the next seven years trying to walk again. He often stayed at a spa in Warm Springs, Georgia, exercising his muscles in therapeutic pools filled with the area's natural mineral waters. In 1926 he bought the property and turned it into a care center open to all polio survivors. Though he never was able to walk without leg braces, he regained much of his strength.

Many who knew Roosevelt believed his struggle with polio transformed him. Frances Perkins, who would become his secretary of labor, said that his pain and suffering purged any arrogance in his attitude. She noted that he emerged

Roosevelt (center) receives physical therapy in an indoor pool at Warm Springs, Georgia, in 1928. His personal struggle with polio led him to open the spa as a care center for others who had suffered from this disease.

"completely warmhearted, with humility of spirit and with a deeper philosophy."

By 1928, when the Democratic Party asked him to run for governor of New York, Franklin Delano Roosevelt was ready to return to politics. He won the election by a very small margin, but it was an important victory that resurrected his political career.

★ CHAPTER TWO ★

ACT NOW
FOR
REFORM

The 1920s had been an era of prosperity like none other in the United States. As the economy grew, stock prices soared. People from all walks of life bought stocks—small portions of ownership in corporations—hoping for a share in the new wealth. Many borrowed money from banks to purchase stocks and then used the possible future value of their stocks to buy homes, cars, and luxury appliances. The result was an unstable economy.

Roosevelt was in the second year of his term as governor of New York when the stock market crashed. On October 24, 1929, a sharp drop in stock prices led to a financial panic. Americans sold their stocks to get whatever value remained. The day became known as Black Thursday. In the following weeks, the market plunged lower and lower, spiraling out of control.

The effects of the stock market crash rippled across the economy. Banks failed, businesses closed, people lost their jobs and homes, and farmers lost their farms. Without work, many Americans went hungry. The United States—and much of the world—descended into the Great Depression.

HOOVER'S TRICKLE-DOWN ECONOMICS

By this time, Republican Herbert Hoover had followed Harding as president. To prevent factories from closing, Hoover tried to protect American industry by raising tariffs (taxes) on foreign goods. But these tariffs raised prices on American goods, which slowed growth. Hoover used federal money to stabilize banks, on the theory that as the banks recovered, that money would trickle down to the people, but the effort was unsuccessful. At a time when modern programs such as welfare did not exist, Hoover didn't want to give money directly to the unemployed and the hungry, feeling this would make them too dependent on government. Hoover believed in voluntary cooperation between groups and individuals, as opposed to government intervention. He believed business and the free market would eventually heal the economy on their own.

Unemployed men line up to receive free food in 1932. Breadlines were often arranged by volunteers rather than by the government.

These policies led many Americans to perceive Hoover as cold and uncaring. The poor turned their empty pockets inside out and called them Hoover flags. Those who could not afford to keep their homes built shacks in areas they called Hoovervilles.

Roosevelt disagreed with Hoover's approach. "To those unfortunate citizens," he said, "aid must be extended by Government, not as a matter of charity, but as a matter of social duty." As governor of New York, he set up a Temporary Emergency Relief Administration to provide jobs for the unemployed in his state.

PRESIDENTIAL CANDIDATE

Roosevelt wanted to challenge Hoover for the presidency in the 1932 election. After a hard-fought primary, Roosevelt won the Democratic Party nomination for president. In his acceptance speech, he promised that the federal government would take bold action to help those who were struggling: "I pledge you, I pledge myself, to a new deal for the American people."

The political tides were against Hoover. Thousands of World War I veterans, many of them out of work, had camped out on the National Mall in Washington, DC, demanding an early payment of the bonuses the government had promised for their military service. Hoover refused and ordered federal troops to clear out this "Bonus Army." The clash that followed resulted in several casualties, including the death of a baby. When Roosevelt heard about what Hoover had done, he told an adviser, "Well, this will elect me."

Roosevelt was right. In November 1932, he defeated Hoover by a landslide, winning forty-two out of forty-eight states. He returned home from campaign headquarters and told his mother that it had been the greatest night in his life. But later, when his grown son James helped him into bed, Roosevelt confessed, "I'm just afraid that I may not have the strength to do this job."

ROOSEVELT AND THE PRESS

From his days as a Harvard reporter, Franklin understood the press, and as a politician, he was able to develop a good relationship with journalists. Roosevelt could walk only a few steps with his leg braces and otherwise relied on a wheelchair. He asked that members of the press never show his disability to the American people. The press generally honored his request. (Members of the Secret Service were known to seize the cameras and film of journalists who did not.) Instead, they often photographed him in his open touring car, which was modified so Roosevelt could drive it with his hands, his fedora hat perched on his head and a smile on his face.

Roosevelt drives his Model A Ford Roadster around Hyde Park in 1933.

THE NEW DEAL

By the time Roosevelt took office four months later, the Depression had deepened. The stock market had plummeted to record lows. The federal government didn't have enough money to pay its employees. Many people had pulled their savings out of banks, forcing banks across the nation to shut down.

Standing on the steps of the Capitol at his inauguration on March 4, 1933, Roosevelt thrust out his chin and looked gravely at the assembled crowd he was about to address. "This great nation will endure as it has endured, will revive and will prosper," he said. "The only thing we have to fear is fear itself. . . . This nation asks for action, and action now." Through the radio, his words reached across America.

Roosevelt delivers his inaugural address from the Capitol steps on March 4, 1933.

BANK HOLIDAYS

At one o'clock in the afternoon on the Monday after his inauguration, Roosevelt declared a national bank holiday, suspending all banking transactions for a week. The goal was to give the volatile banking industry a chance to stabilize— and to calm Americans' fears about the safety of keeping their money in banks. The measure didn't greatly change the situation since so many states had already closed their banks. All the same, it signaled that the federal government was taking control.

Roosevelt consulted with his economic advisers and the nation's governors. They helped him create the Emergency Banking Act. The act passed so quickly through a special session of Congress that most senators and representatives didn't even have a chance to read it. The law gave the government a far greater level of oversight over banks nationwide, including the power to shut down weak or unstable banks.

Over the radio, in the first of what would become known as Fireside Chats, the president explained what he was doing and why. He assured Americans that "it is safer to keep your money in a reopened bank than under the mattress." People listened. When the banks reopened on March 13, 1933, customers gathered in long lines to return their savings to banks.

THE THREE Rs

Over the next one hundred days, Roosevelt pushed through more legislation than Congress had passed in any other previous period in history. Many of his new programs became known by their initials. In fact, Americans were soon calling the president himself by his initials, FDR. To get the nation back on its feet, Roosevelt concentrated on three Rs: relief, reform, and recovery.

FIRESIDE CHATS

Roosevelt made expert use of radio, the main broadcast medium in the days before the spread of television. At crucial moments in his presidency, Roosevelt would speak directly on radio to the American people, addressing them as "my friends," and using simple language to clearly explain what was happening. These talks became known as Fireside Chats. Roosevelt gave thirty Fireside Chats during his presidency.

Roosevelt delivers his first Fireside Chat on March 12, 1933.

His reform programs were geared to adjust the way banks and other businesses operated. The goal was not only to help the nation climb out of the Great Depression but to make sure a similar event could never happen again. One of Roosevelt's key pieces of legislation was the Securities Act of 1933. It stipulated that whenever a stock, a bond, or another investment was offered for sale, the seller had to give investors all significant information about it. The law also required that this information be accurate, without misrepresentation or fraud. The government established the Securities and Exchange Commission (SEC) to regulate the commerce of the stock market.

GOLD STANDARD

When Roosevelt took office, the US dollar was still on the gold standard. This meant that all US currency was worth a certain amount of gold. The actual gold was kept in storage by the Federal Reserve, the United States' central banking system, but Americans could cash in coins and paper bills for the precious metal.

During the Great Depression, faith in the US banking system had collapsed. Many Americans turned to hoarding gold. They cashed in bank notes for the valuable metal, which drained federal gold stores. At first, Roosevelt was unsure how to deal with the situation. When questioned by the press, he hedged his answers. "For a good long time, as a matter of actual fact, the United States has been the only country on the gold standard," he noted.

Roosevelt consulted with his advisers about abandoning the gold standard. Most were against this, but one, George Warren, urged him to go ahead. Roosevelt's other economic advisers were furious when they found out what he intended to do. The assistant secretary to the treasury resigned. Roosevelt went ahead with his plans anyway.

29

On April 5, 1933, Roosevelt issued an executive order requiring Americans to turn in their gold in exchange for other currency. Banks were prohibited from paying out gold or exporting it to other countries. This increased the amount of gold held by the Federal Reserve, which boosted the value of US currency and gave the federal government greater control in stabilizing the economy.

BANKING GUARANTEES

Because so many Americans had lost their life savings to bank failures, they wanted some guarantee that their deposits would be secure in the future. Originally Roosevelt did not want the federal government to provide insurance for bank deposits. His secretary

A crowd gathers outside a bank in 1933. Americans were hesitant to trust banks during the Great Depression. Roosevelt worked hard to ease the public's fears and to stablize the economy.

of the treasury, William Woodin, feared it would be too expensive and would reward bad bank management. But at the urging of his vice president, John Nance Garner, and others in his party, Roosevelt changed his mind. He supported the Glass-Steagall Act, or Banking Act, which established the Federal Deposit Insurance Corporation (FDIC). Through this corporation, the US government would insure any deposit up to $2,500 in a member bank.

During the Great Depression, some banks had failed because they had used depositors' money to invest unwisely in stocks and bonds. The Banking Act created a separation between commercial banks and investment companies, limiting the way banks could invest money and reducing the amount of risk a bank could take with depositors' funds. The act also gave the federal government oversight over all commercial banks. Roosevelt signed the Banking Act into law on June 16, 1933, helping to restore confidence in the banking system.

In his first Fireside Chat, Roosevelt had reminded Americans that the success of these new economic measures depended on them. "There is an element in the readjustment of our financial system more important than currency, more important than gold, and that is the confidence of the people," he said. He urged them, "Let us unite in banishing fear. We have provided the machinery to restore our financial system. It is up to you to support and make it work."

CHAPTER THREE

BACK TO WORK FOR RELIEF

Roosevelt took office at the low point of the Great Depression, when almost one-quarter of the American workforce was unemployed. Unable to pay their mortgages, families were forced out of their homes into shantytowns or onto the streets. Starving, they begged for food or lined up at soup kitchens for free meals. Private charities did not have enough resources to meet the great need, and no government aid programs existed. Roosevelt believed the government should do something to address the people's misery. This would be his New Deal for the nation.

FEDERAL EMERGENCY RELIEF ADMINISTRATION AND THE WORKS PROGRESS ADMINISTRATION

One of the first programs Franklin created was the Federal Emergency Relief Administration (FERA). He selected one of his closest advisers, Harry Hopkins, to run it. The money Congress set aside for the program wouldn't be given directly to people in need. Roosevelt was not in favor of direct relief. He felt it demoralized the people who received it and risked making them dependent on handouts. Instead, FERA money would go to the states to help fund their relief programs.

FERA soon shifted from providing monetary aid to creating work opportunities. Some critics felt that these were just "make-work" projects that would cost the government more money than they were worth. However, in its two years as a program, FERA put fifteen million Americans to work. FERA employees planned and constructed public buildings, libraries, and theaters and improved national parks. FERA funded archaeology projects and research into new products for farming and fishing. It funded vocational training, adult literacy programs, and preschools.

In 1935, the Works Progress Administration (WPA) took the place of FERA. Under the WPA, workers built bridges, roads, public

The Works Progress Administration (WPA) sponsored projects to help Americans find employment. Here, men work on a WPA bridge-spillway project at near Pierre, South Dakota, in July 1936.

buildings, parks, and airports, all for an average monthly salary of $41.57. This was a fairly low wage, since the average salary of an industrial worker at the time was about $85 a month. All the same, these Americans were thrilled to have jobs to help support their families. WPA programs also employed workers to care for the elderly, watch children in nursery schools, and prepare and serve food at school lunch programs. These jobs were usually filled by women.

Prominent members of the arts community wanted the WPA to expand to include programs for painters and other artists. According to Frances Perkins, a young girl who was related to one of Roosevelt's cabinet members suggested this idea to the

WPA artists work on a mural commissioned for a public building in Central Park in New York City, 1935.

THE DUST BOWL

From 1930 to 1940, the Great Plains west of the Missouri River and east of the Rocky Mountains suffered a severe drought. Soil—bare from a lack of rainfall, overfarming, and overgrazing—dried up and blew away, creating billowing clouds of dust that could darken the sky for days. The fine dust seeped into cracks, covering everything with deep layers of grit. Unable to make a living, many farmers abandoned their land. Thousands of homeless and hungry families headed west to California, seeking jobs. There, many Americans worked as day laborers on large farms run by corporations. The work paid very little and was almost always temporary. People moved from one corporate farm to another, living in crowded camps with no plumbing and makeshift shelters.

president. Roosevelt responded, "Why not? They are human beings. They have to live." So at the standard rate of fifteen dollars a week, artists were hired to paint murals and create sculptures for public buildings across the nation. The program later expanded to include writing, music, theater, and historical research as well. WPA arts projects ranged from publishing cookbooks of regional recipes to recording oral histories of former slaves.

THE CIVILIAN CONSERVATION CORPS

The Civilian Conservation Corps (CCC) was another New Deal program. Roosevelt proposed that the nation recruit its unemployed young men into a peacetime "army" to work on

environmental projects, such as battling erosion and protecting the country's natural resources.

The CCC's goal was to employ 250,000 young men, between the ages of eighteen and twenty-five, and to do it within a few months. Roosevelt tapped the War Department (the present-day Department of Defense) to organize the enrollees and relocate them to CCC camps around the nation. The Department of the Interior and the Department of Agriculture were responsible for constructing the CCC camps and supervising the projects. The Department of Labor was responsible for selecting candidates for the program.

The CCC worked on a wide range of projects. Employees created drainage systems to protect farmland from water erosion. They helped stop erosion on more than 20 million acres (8 million hectares) of land. Workers replanted deforested areas. They also built parks and recreation facilities and fire towers.

The effects of the Great Depression were deeply felt on American Indian reservations too, where poverty was rampant. Reservation land suffered from severe drought and erosion, which meant farming was almost impossible. The CCC included an entire division dedicated to giving American Indians jobs restoring their lands.

The CCC also played a role with returning military veterans. In 1933, a second Bonus Army marched on Washington, led by unemployed veterans who wanted to see what the new president would do for them. Roosevelt didn't send troops to drive them out, as Hoover had. Instead, Roosevelt sent Eleanor. The vets gave her a tour of the camp. They shared their noon meal with her, and she led them in songs. Then she returned to the White House and reported to her husband on what she had seen and heard. In response, the president offered the vets jobs with the CCC.

Eventually, more than five hundred thousand boys and men worked in CCC camps across every state in the

Members of the Civilian Conservation Corps (CCC) transplant trees in 1933. The program put young men to work on environmental projects.

nation. The CCC also provided employees with education and vocational training. Roosevelt summed up all that the CCC had accomplished in a radio address of April 26, 1933: "Although many of you entered the camps undernourished and discouraged . . . the hard work, regular hours, the plain, wholesome food, and the outdoor life of the CCC camps brought . . . improved morale. As muscles hardened . . . you grasped the opportunity to learn by practical training on the job and through camp educational facilities."

The CCC was popular among both Democrats and Republicans. When Roosevelt attempted to cut its funding to limit the rising costs of his New Deal programs, the American people protested and Congress refused his request. Roosevelt was forced to leave the CCC's budget intact.

ELEANOR ROOSEVELT

Eleanor was the most active First Lady in American history. As a single young woman, she had volunteered at a settlement house in New York City, helping poor immigrants. When she first married, Eleanor gave up that work to be a traditional wife and mother. She entertained Franklin's political guests but otherwise stayed in the background of his career. Gradually, she began to take a greater role outside the home, attending legislative sessions when Franklin was a New York senator and volunteering with the Red Cross during World War I.

After she learned of Roosevelt's affair with Lucy Mercer, Eleanor's relationship with her husband changed. No longer a romantic couple, the two developed a strong working partnership. Franklin's political adviser, Louis Howe, coached Eleanor on politics and public speaking. After Franklin developed polio, Louis and Eleanor both urged him to continue his political career.

Eleanor eventually became a politician in her own right, active in the League of Women Voters and the women's

Eleanor attends an event in Virginia on August 12, 1933.

division of the New York Democratic Party. She wrote magazine and newspaper columns and spoke on the radio. She held regular press conferences and allowed only women reporters to attend them, forcing news organizations to hire more women.

Eleanor also reached out directly to the public, inviting Americans to write to her and connecting people in need to agencies that could help them. She brought Americans' concerns to the attention of her husband, lobbying particularly for civil rights for women, African Americans, youth, and unemployed coal miners. She also traveled extensively, inspecting New Deal programs, visiting soldiers, and representing the Roosevelt administration across the nation.

Eleanor visits a WPA work site in Des Moines, Iowa, in 1936. The project converted a city dump into a waterfront park.

THE TENNESSEE VALLEY AUTHORITY

Before the early 1930s, the Tennessee Valley was one of the poorest areas in the country. Extending across the entire state of Tennessee as well as parts of Kentucky, Mississippi, Alabama, Georgia, North Carolina, and Virginia, it was a difficult place for farmers to make a living. Its fields had been overfarmed. Its topsoil was eroded and its nutrients depleted. The area also regularly flooded.

Roosevelt asked Nebraska Republican senator George Norris to come up with a program to address the area's problems. Norris developed the basic idea for the Tennessee Valley Authority (TVA).

The Tennessee River often flooded farms and communities in the Tennessee Valley. To combat this problem, the Tennessee Valley Authority (TVA) employed workers to build dams along the river.

Then Roosevelt asked Congress to create "a corporation clothed with the power of government but possessed of the flexibility and initiative of private enterprise." They agreed to do so.

The TVA built dams across the Tennessee River to improve navigation, control floods, reduce erosion, and provide water power for electricity. TVA programs reforested bare slopes, taught farmers better methods of growing crops, and set up programs to control the spread of malaria.

Not everyone supported Roosevelt's TVA program. The most controversial aspect of the TVA was its production and sale of electricity. Several private power companies filed lawsuits against the TVA, claiming the government program had no right to compete with their services. They challenged the government's right to produce electrical power. The courts ruled in favor of the TVA.

SOCIAL SECURITY

Roosevelt also wanted to provide for the elderly and others who were unable to work. These people had no safety net. They relied on their families and friends for support, or they went without. The president envisioned a program that would help. It would work like an insurance policy. People would contribute money from their paychecks during the years that they worked. Then, when someone retired or became unable to work, he or she would receive money from the program. The more money someone contributed, the more that person would receive in benefits later. Roosevelt put secretary of labor Frances Perkins in charge of designing the program. Based on testimony from business leaders, labor officials, and academic experts, Perkins's committee hammered out a plan to fund the program with a combination of individual payroll contributions and taxes. The program eventually became known as Social Security.

Secretary of labor Frances Perkins explains the design of the new Social Security program in front of a congressional committee on January 22, 1935.

Roosevelt had hoped for a "cradle to grave" package that would include health care too. Opponents worried that the measure would be the first step toward socialistic control, in which the government, rather than private business, controls industry. Roosevelt's big-government New Deal programs—and their costs—were piling up. His critics became increasingly concerned that the president was making Americans too reliant on their government.

Nevertheless, the law creating Social Security passed Congress by a large margin. It provided unemployment insurance, accident and disability benefits, support for dependent children, and old-age benefits. When he signed the bill into law on August 14, 1935, Roosevelt explained, "We have tried to frame a law which

will give some measure of protection to the average citizen and to his family against the loss of a job and against poverty-ridden old age. . . . If the Senate and the House of Representatives . . . had done nothing more than pass this bill, the session would be regarded as historic for all time."

Many of the New Deal programs were experimental, and Roosevelt wanted to know what was working and what wasn't. Eleanor became his eyes, ears, and legs, traveling the country to observe conditions and report back to him. He told her to notice people's faces, their cars, and the condition of their clothes. Whenever she returned, he would grill her, asking what people had to eat and how they lived. He would appear at his next cabinet meeting to report, "My missus says . . ."

CHAPTER FOUR

COOPERATE

FOR

RECOVERY

The Great Depression hit farmers hard. They faced low prices for their crops and a major drought. Within his first few weeks in office, Roosevelt turned his attention to the farmers' situation.

Part of the problem was oversupply. American agriculture grew more food than the country needed, causing prices to drop so drastically that crops cost more to grow than farmers could earn by selling them. So farmers stopped harvesting their crops, and food rotted in the fields. Farmers who couldn't pay their mortgages lost their land. Those who had rented land could no longer afford the payments and were forced to wander the countryside, desperate for work.

THE AGRICULTURAL ADJUSTMENT ACT

To break this dismal cycle, Franklin gathered a group to brainstorm legislation that addressed agricultural problems. He told the editor of the newspaper *Prairie Farmer*, "I am going to call farmers' leaders together, lock them in a room, and tell them not to come out until they have agreed on a plan."

Low grain prices and drought caused problems for farmers during the 1930s. As crops failed, many farmers struggled to make a living.

The group considered a plan that would let the government set prices for crops. Another suggestion involved allowing the US government to buy up the country's entire surplus. The group rejected both ideas and, after much debate, came up with the Agricultural Adjustment Act (AAA). This bill, which Congress passed in May 1933, paid farmers not to grow oversupplied crops, such as wheat, corn, and cotton.

As Roosevelt explained, this would be "a plan for the adjustment of totals in our major crops, so that from year to year production and consumption would be kept in reasonable balance with each other, to the end that reasonable prices would be paid to farmers for their crops." A newly created Agricultural Adjustment Administration decided how much of each crop farmers should produce. The government would purchase some of the excess crops and sell them overseas.

WARM SPRINGS AND THE GEORGIA FARMERS

Franklin Roosevelt had originally stayed at the spa in Warm Springs, Georgia, to recover from polio. He eventually bought the spa, where he would retreat to relax and refresh throughout his presidency. He often toured the Georgia countryside, getting to know the local farmers and talking to them about their problems. The insights he gained guided him in framing the Agricultural Adjustment Act and many of his other New Deal strategies.

Roosevelt stops to shake hands with a farmer while on his way to Warm Springs in October 1932. Roosevelt frequently met with farmers to discuss their struggles.

The bill was controversial because it paid farmers to destroy some of their surplus crops and livestock. This idea didn't sit well with people when so many Americans were hungry. Some argued that big growers would benefit more from this program than the small family farmer. Some said that tenant farmers who labored on other people's farms would actually be worse off, since farmers with fewer crops to harvest hired less help. Most farmers benefited, however. Without oversupply, crop and livestock prices began to rise, and farmers saw their income double between 1932 and 1936.

Two Alabama farmers compare cotton prices disributed as part of the Agricultural Adjustment Act.

The program ended in 1936, when the Supreme Court declared that the AAA was unconstitutional because regulation of agriculture was a state power. A new Agricultural Adjustment Act, which addressed the Supreme Court's objections, was passed in 1938, though it wasn't as effective at dealing with surpluses.

THE NATIONAL RECOVERY ADMINISTRATION

To boost the nation's economic recovery, Roosevelt wanted to regulate industry as well as agriculture. He asked various business groups to come up with suggestions. As a model, he pointed to the War Industries Board, which had overseen industry during World War I.

The president emphasized the importance of protecting industrial workers' needs. In a 1933 talk before the US Chamber of Commerce, Roosevelt said that the majority of industries were "willing to work together to prevent overproduction, to prevent unfair wages, and to eliminate improper working conditions." He pointed out to the business leaders, "It is ultimately of little [use] to any of you to be temporarily prosperous while others are permanently depressed," and he urged them to "lay aside special and selfish interests, to think of and act for a well-rounded national recovery."

The result was the National Recovery Administration (NRA). The 1933 act that created the NRA directed each industry to draw up agreements regulating prices, production levels, and working conditions. Workers would be guaranteed the right to organize and join labor unions to address fair pay and working conditions. The act also required participating industries to establish maximum workweeks of thirty-five to forty hours and minimum wages of twelve to fifteen dollars a week. Any industry that followed the NRA standards had the right to display a Blue Eagle logo on its label. Consumers were encouraged to support Blue Eagle products.

Roosevelt (seated) signs the National Industrial Recovery Act on June 16, 1933. This bill created the National Recovery Administration to regulate and improve industry.

The NRA was successful in regulating some labor practices. For example, it ended child labor in the textile industry. But it was unable to enforce many of its own rules. In addition, small businesses complained that the NRA favored big businesses. Labor leaders complained that it favored employers. Critics also complained about price fixing, claiming that this led to higher prices for many products and therefore hurt consumers. In 1935 the Supreme Court declared the law unconstitutional.

In response, Congress passed the Wagner Act to restore laborers' right to organize and to engage in collective bargaining, or negotiations with their employers. To protect that right, Congress established the National Labor Relations Board. When he signed the Wagner Act into law, Roosevelt said, "A better relationship between labor and management is the high purpose

FAIR LABOR STANDARDS ACT OF 1938

The NRA was only Roosevelt's first step toward establishing fair workplace conditions for Americans. He took further steps with the Fair Labor Standards Act of 1938, which set more sweeping regulations for working conditions, including the first national minimum wage (twenty-five cents per hour) and the first national maximum workweek (forty-four hours). Roosevelt pushed hard for the controversial bill, which went through several rounds of debate and revisions before gaining congressional approval a year after it was first introduced.

of this Act. By assuring the employees the right of collective bargaining it fosters the development of the employment contract on a sound and [fair] basis."

BLACK MONDAY AND PACKING THE COURT

Conservative critics argued that Roosevelt's New Deal programs restricted capitalism (private ownership of business) and free enterprise (competition among businesses). They won a legal victory on what became known as Black Monday. On that day, May 27, 1935, the Supreme Court ruled against several Roosevelt policies, including a law that aimed to help farmers struggling to pay their mortgages. Supreme Court decisions stated that the US government was overstepping its constitutional powers by taking over decisions that states and private organizations should make.

Roosevelt was infuriated. Most of the nine Supreme Court judges had been appointed by previous conservative Republican

presidents. Roosevelt asked Congress to give him the right to appoint three more judges to the court, for a total of twelve. But Congress rejected this move to "pack the court" as another case of Roosevelt overstepping presidential powers.

THE 1936 PRESIDENTIAL CAMPAIGN

By this time, the New Deal was losing popularity. Roosevelt's opponents raised their voices as the 1936 elections approached. Those on the political right charged him with strangling free enterprise and turning the country into a welfare state. Critics pointed to the growing national debt. When Roosevelt raised taxes on the wealthy to pay for his New Deal programs, he was

A crowd listens as Roosevelt (center left) gives a campaign speech from the back of a train in 1936.

called a traitor to his class. Meanwhile, many on the political left thought he hadn't done enough to help the downtrodden.

In his campaign speeches, Roosevelt addressed his critics. He pointed out that he had saved a democratic free enterprise system on the brink of ruin: "Because we cherished our system of private property and free enterprise and were determined to preserve it as the foundation of our traditional American system, we recalled the warning of Thomas Jefferson that 'widespread poverty and concentrated wealth cannot long endure side by side in a democracy.'"

THE ROOSEVELT RECESSION

In Roosevelt's first term as president, the United States had made progress in rising out of the Great Depression. Investment was increasing, consumer sales were up, and unemployment was down. Then the economy suffered another slump in 1937. The stock market plunged, and unemployment rose for the first time since Roosevelt became president. Critics blamed the reversal on Roosevelt's decision to cut government spending and allow many of his experimental programs to end. As these programs shut down, the people they had employed found themselves out of work. Unemployed Americans spent less money, which led to a downturn in the economy. Concerned by this turn of events, Roosevelt increased spending again in 1938, and unemployment soon fell. The thirteen-month slump became known as the Roosevelt Recession.

Roosevelt signs bills in the Oval Office in 1936.

Roosevelt had halted the banking crisis and put millions to work. The income of farmers had doubled during his presidency. Most Americans trusted him. He was the president of the Fireside Chat, who spoke directly to his people. In 1936 he was reelected with 60.8 percent of the vote, decisively defeating Republican Alfred Landon. He won forty-six of the forty-eight states, the largest margin of victory in the history of US presidential elections, and his party won a landslide majority of seats in Congress.

★ CHAPTER FIVE ★

TIDES
OF
WAR

In 1933, the year that Roosevelt began his first term, Adolf Hitler had become chancellor of Germany. The nation had been struggling to rise from a humiliating defeat in World War I. During the global depression, Germans suffered terribly. Hitler came to power by promising a better economic future in a glorious new German empire, which he called the Third Reich. Hitler and his Nazi Party also appealed to many Germans' hatred and fear of Jews and other minorities by blaming them for the country's problems.

Hitler was influenced by Benito Mussolini, the leader of a political movement called fascism, who had declared himself dictator of Italy in 1925. Mussolini wrote that Fascists didn't believe in the possibility or usefulness of peace: "For Fascism, the growth of empire, that is to say the expansion of the nation, is an essential [display] of vitality, and its opposite a sign of [decline]." Mussolini hoped to return Italy to its ancient glory days as a major European power.

On the other side of the world, Japanese military leaders were drawing up plans for what they called the Greater East Asia

Co-Prosperity Sphere. Their goal was to expel Western influences from Asia and establish Japan as the continent's dominant power. Japan had occupied Korea in 1910, and in 1931, it invaded Manchuria, a region in northeastern China.

Adolf Hitler (front center) stands with members of his Nazi Party in 1933. Hitler's rise to power concerned world leaders.

NEUTRALITY ACT

The horrors of World War I remained fresh in the minds of Americans. Most were isolationists who didn't want to get involved in the troubles of other nations. Roosevelt understood, having visited the war's battlefields during his term as assistant secretary of the navy. "I have seen war," he said in an address at Chautauqua, New York. "I have seen blood running from the wounded. . . . I have seen children starving. . . . I hate war." But Roosevelt felt the United States would eventually need to take a role in the growing conflict of the 1930s.

In 1935 Congress passed the Neutrality Act, prohibiting the United States from exporting weapons to nations at war. Roosevelt opposed the embargo, but at the time he was more concerned about pushing legislation to establish Social Security and the WPA. Under pressure from the American public, he signed the Neutrality Act into law. Congress renewed the act in 1936, adding language that forbade the United States from making loans to nations at war.

RISE OF THE AXIS POWERS

Meanwhile, Germany, Italy, and Japan signed a series of treaties agreeing that world power should rotate around their axis: Germany in Europe, Italy in the Mediterranean, and Japan in the Pacific. The three countries became known as the Axis powers.

In 1935 Mussolini invaded Ethiopia, then called Abyssinia, incorporating the African nation into his new Italian empire. In 1937 Japan went to war with China. The following year, Hitler seized Austria and western Czechoslovakia (present-day Czech Republic and Slovakia). He signed a treaty with the United Kingdom and France, promising that this was his last territorial demand. Six months later, however, Hitler invaded the rest of Czechoslovakia.

Roosevelt watched these developments with alarm. In a 1937 speech at a gathering of his supporters in Chicago, Illinois, Roosevelt denounced the international lawlessness that rained bombs on innocent civilians. He predicted that if the violence continued, every part of the world would suffer. "Let no one imagine that America will escape," he warned. The public's reaction to this speech was mixed, and isolationists were offended by Roosevelt's message.

THREAT TO EUROPEAN JEWS

On November 9, 1938, the Nazis unleashed Kristallnacht, "the night of broken glass," an organized attack on Jews throughout Germany and German-occupied lands. Nazi Party members and other Germans destroyed thousands of synagogues and many more Jewish homes and businesses. Officials rounded up as many as thirty thousand Jewish men and sent them to concentration camps, where Jews and other minorities were imprisoned and systematically murdered.

Though the details of the concentration camps were not yet widely known, Kristallnacht shocked and horrified the American people. Roosevelt declared, "I myself could scarcely believe that such things could occur in a twentieth-century civilization." In protest, he immediately pulled the American ambassador out of Germany.

Eleanor Roosevelt urged the president to support a bill in Congress that would allow twenty thousand German Jewish refugee children into the country. Roosevelt doubted it would pass. The United States set immigration quotas, or limits, for people of specific nationalities, and the quota for German immigrants had already been filled that year. Furthermore, the majority of Americans were anti-immigration, and many were

Local residents watch as a synagogue burns during Kristallnacht in Ober-Ramstadt, Germany. It was one of many attacks against Jews conducted by Nazis during the late 1930s.

anti-Semitic. In fact, a 1939 opinion poll recorded that 53 percent of Americans surveyed believed "Jews are different and should be restricted" from entering the United States. In any case, with US unemployment still high, many Americans felt that new immigrants would compete with Americans for jobs.

With all this in mind, Roosevelt chose not to push for increased quotas for Jewish immigrants. Instead, he issued an executive order allowing German Jews who were already in the United States to stay longer. This saved the lives of about fifteen thousand Jews, a small number compared to the millions of European Jews who were eventually murdered in Nazi concentration camps.

CASH-AND-CARRY LAW

In September 1939, Hitler invaded Poland. In response, Britain and France declared war against Germany, officially igniting World War II in Europe. In rapid succession, Germany took over Norway, Denmark, Belgium, and the Netherlands. Then Germany attacked France, which it occupied in 1940.

On September 3, 1939, Roosevelt warned Americans during a Fireside Chat, "When peace has been broken anywhere, the peace of all countries everywhere is in danger. It is easy for you and for me to shrug our shoulders . . . [at] conflicts taking place thousands of miles from the continental United States. . . . Passionately though we may desire detachment, we are forced to realize that every word that comes through the air, every ship that sails the sea, every battle that is fought, does affect the American future."

Britain and France were desperate for weapons, but under the Neutrality Act, the United States couldn't supply them. Roosevelt lobbied Congress to have the embargo on arms sales repealed. At first, Congress refused. In November 1939, after much debate, Congress allowed cash-and-carry arms sales. This

meant Britain and France could buy weapons from the United
States if they paid cash.

PRESIDENTIAL ELECTION 1940

In response to the cash-and-carry policy, isolationists held rallies
demanding the country return to its neutral stance. Roosevelt
declared he would run for a third term—the first time any
president in US history had done so. The possibility of American
involvement in the war became a major issue in the campaign.

After France fell, Britain was the last holdout facing the
Nazi onslaught in Europe. The Germans had overrun all other
Western European nations except a handful of neutral countries.
In September 1940 Germany launched nightly bombing raids on

*Roosevelt and Winston Churchill, prime minister of Great Britain, meet in
August 1941. The two worked closely as allies during World War II.*

Britain's major cities, while its submarines relentlessly attacked British ships. British prime minister, Winston Churchill, begged Roosevelt to send warships to combat the German submarines. Roosevelt knew that if he agreed, the decision could endanger his reelection. All the same, he told his personal secretary, Grace Tully, he had to do it: "Even another day's delay may mean the end of civilization." By executive order—bypassing congressional approval—he transferred fifty old but seaworthy destroyers to Britain. In exchange, the United States received several British bases. In response, Roosevelt's Republican opponent in the 1940 presidential race, Wendell Willkie, accused the president of being dictatorial and arbitrary. Voters didn't seem to mind. In November of 1940, they turned out for the presidential election in record numbers. Roosevelt was elected to a third term by a large margin, taking thirty-eight of the nation's forty-eight states.

TERM LIMITS

Until the late 1940s, the US Constitution did not limit the number of terms a president could serve. The nation's first president, George Washington, had been asked to run for a third time but decided against it. FDR became the only president to serve more than two terms. In response to this lengthy presidency, Congress passed the Twenty-Second Amendment to the US Constitution in 1947. The amendment went into effect in 1951 and limits a president to two terms in office.

Roosevelt waves to supporters on November 4, 1940, the evening before voters elected him to a historic third term.

LEND-LEASE ACT

After the election, Roosevelt appealed to Congress to end the arms embargo. Britain was out of money, unable to pay cash for weapons it desperately needed. In a Fireside Chat just after Christmas 1940, Roosevelt explained, "The British people and their allies today are conducting an active war against this unholy alliance [the Axis powers]. Our own future security is greatly dependent on the outcome of that fight. Our ability to 'keep out of war' is going to be affected by that outcome." He told Americans that to avoid war, the US government must provide aid to those who were fighting. "We must be the great arsenal of democracy," he said. A few months later, in March 1941, Roosevelt convinced Congress to pass the Lend-Lease Act. This policy allowed the United States to temporarily provide war supplies to any nation whose defense was considered vital to US national security.

THE FOUR FREEDOMS

In his January 6, 1941, State of the Union address, Roosevelt told the country that it stood at a pivotal moment in history. American security was under greater threat than ever before. To impress upon Americans the global magnitude of events playing out overseas, Roosevelt spelled out the four freedoms he felt were essential to all citizens of the world. He said:

In the future days, which we seek to make secure, we look forward to a world founded upon four essential human freedoms.

The first is freedom of speech and expression—everywhere in the world.

The second is freedom of every person to worship God in his own way—everywhere in the world.

The third is freedom from want, which, translated into world terms, means economic understandings which will secure to every nation a healthy peacetime life for its inhabitants—everywhere in the world.

The fourth is freedom from fear, which, translated into world terms, means a world-wide reduction of armaments to such a point and in such a thorough fashion that no nation will be in a position to commit an act of physical aggression against any neighbor—anywhere in the world.

ESCALATING AGGRESSION

In June 1941, Germany invaded the Soviet Union (fifteen republics that included Russia), breaking a nonaggression pact the two nations had signed in 1939. As a result, the Soviet leader, Joseph Stalin, became an uneasy member of the Allied forces.

In Asia, European countries held large spheres of influence— areas where a nation has more power than others to direct culture, government, and economic matters. Europe's main spheres of influence were in China, British Malaya (part of present-day Malaysia), and Dutch Indonesia (present-day Indonesia). The United States held influence over the Philippines, which had been a US colony until 1935, and over several Pacific islands, as well. Japanese leaders sought to drive out foreigners and take control of Asia themselves. In 1937 Japan invaded China, and in 1940, it attacked French Indochina (parts of present-day Vietnam, Cambodia, and Laos). Roosevelt responded by ordering a limited trade embargo against Japan.

Since Japan had few natural resources, its military depended on outside supplies to wage war. To gain control of rubber, oil, and other raw materials they needed, the Japanese would have to quickly conquer British and Dutch colonies in Southeast Asia, where these materials were plentiful. Japanese military leaders believed the only force that could stop them was the American Pacific fleet, headquartered at Pearl Harbor, Hawaii. They prepared to attack the American naval base at Pearl Harbor.

★ CHAPTER SIX ★

FIGHT
FOR
FREEDOM

The Japanese attack on Pearl Harbor on December 7, 1941, was a crushing blow to the United States. More than two thousand Americans lost their lives, while numerous ships and aircraft were damaged or destroyed.

At Roosevelt's urging, Congress quickly passed a declaration of war against Japan. Four days after Pearl Harbor, Germany declared war on the United States. Congress unanimously approved a resolution declaring war on Germany and its fellow Axis nations. With these declarations, the United States officially joined Britain, the Soviet Union, and their supporters as a member of the Allied forces.

THE INTERNMENT OF JAPANESE AMERICANS

After the attack on Pearl Harbor, anti-Japanese feelings ran high. This was especially true along the West Coast, which was home to tens of thousands of Japanese Americans. Secretary of war Henry Stimson told Roosevelt that the Japanese might invade the West Coast of the United States—and that Japanese Americans might aid the enemy by spying or by sabotaging the

US military. He recommended that all US citizens of Japanese descent, as well as recent immigrants from Japan, be placed in internment camps.

The president agreed that relocating Japanese Americans was a "military necessity." He took a hands-off approach to the issue, leaving the details to Stimson, though he urged, "Be as reasonable as you can."

The president's executive order of February 19, 1942, authorized the secretary of war to create protected military areas along the Pacific coast. Anyone who was considered a threat to US security could be kept out of these areas. Because the newly designated military areas included many West Coast cities, more than 110,000 Japanese American men, women, and

Japanese men, women, and children crowd a street at an internment camp in Rivers, Arizona. These types of camps housed more than 110,000 people, most whom were American citizens, during the war.

children—as well as about 5,000 Germans and 300 Italians—were forced to leave their homes. The US government set up internment camps where these people lived during the war years. About 70 percent of the internees were American citizens, and none was ever charged with a crime. Most were allowed to take only a few possessions with them and had to leave their homes quickly, with no time to sell or store valuables, businesses, or other property.

When the camps were eventually disbanded in 1945, most internees returned to the cities where they had lived before the war and worked to rebuild their lives. Decades later, the United States formally apologized for the internment and agreed to pay monetary compensation to survivors. According to the Civil Liberties act of 1988, the internment "was caused by race prejudice, war hysteria, and a failure of political leadership."

EXPANDING WAR

Meanwhile, Roosevelt turned his attention to the war effort. In December 1941, Winston Churchill traveled to Washington, DC, where he met with Roosevelt to plan their mutual defense. The British prime minister stayed for three weeks, and the two leaders became close friends. Churchill often sauntered into Roosevelt's bedroom, or Roosevelt would roll his wheelchair into Churchill's room, to discuss plans over breakfast.

Roosevelt's top priority was to strengthen the US military. The attack on Pearl Harbor had disabled a large portion of the US Pacific fleet. The remaining vessels were not enough to match the Japanese forces. The United States needed more ships—as well as more planes, tanks, and weapons. That would mean increasing American war production.

In his 1942 annual budget message, he told Americans that they would need to sacrifice in the years ahead. Victory would

ELEANOR ROOSEVELT AND WORLD WAR II

Throughout the war, Eleanor remained one of Roosevelt's most valued advisers. She crisscrossed the globe, visiting troops on three continents, trudging through the mud to visit the wounded, and taking notes on morale and conditions to share with her husband. She was a vocal supporter of African American troops and of American women who took jobs to help the war effort. She also urged Roosevelt to keep his New Deal programs running during the war, a stance that was unpopular with some of Roosevelt's other advisers. From Eleanor's perspective, a victory in the global conflict would be meaningless if the United States failed to honor its democratic ideals of fairness and opportunity at home.

not be won only in battle but in the mines, in the shops, and on the farms. All production would be focused on war needs. He said, "It is not enough to turn out just a few more planes, a few more tanks, a few more guns, a few more ships, than can be turned out by our enemies. We must outproduce [the enemy] overwhelmingly, so that there can be no question of our ability to provide a crushing superiority of equipment."

Roosevelt created the War Production Board to oversee industrial production of war materials. Factories already producing war materials increased their output. Other companies redirected their efforts. For example, instead of manufacturing cars, Ford Motors made B-24 bombers. General Motors made airplane engines, guns, trucks, and tanks.

Roosevelt's New Deal programs had never completely eliminated unemployment. With war production ramped up, unemployment essentially disappeared by 1944. In fact, with so many men serving in the armed services, women took on jobs usually reserved for men. They became vital contributors to the war effort, assembling engines, building bombers, and manufacturing weapons.

To pay for the war, Roosevelt raised taxes. He also urged Americans to buy war bonds—a type of loan to the US government—to show their patriotism. The government limited the sale of goods such as rubber, metal, clothing, sugar, meat, cooking oil, and canned goods. These items were essential to building weapons and feeding and clothing the nation's soldiers.

The war effort brought an increased need for American workers. Many women entered the workforce to meet industry's demands.

SELECTIVE SERVICE

The Selective Training and Service Act of 1940 required all men between the ages of twenty-one and forty-five to register for the draft. Eventually ten million American men were drafted into the armed services to serve during World War II. Women were not drafted during World War II. Instead, nearly 350,000 women served in the armed forces as volunteers.

Price controls on these goods held down inflation, preventing a steep rise in their cost.

ALLIED VICTORIES AND TENSIONS

As the United States built up its arsenal, the tide of war turned. In June 1942, US code breakers intercepted a message detailing a Japanese plot to invade Midway, a small Pacific atoll (island) housing an American naval base. In response, the US Navy ambushed the Japanese, sinking four Japanese aircraft carriers and foiling the Japanese plans to capture Midway. This was a turning point for the war in the Pacific. US forces began to make steady gains. Meanwhile, Allied troops pushed back the Nazis in North Africa. The Allies also began around-the-clock bombing raids on Germany, and the campaign to take Italy began.

In his Fireside Chat of September 7, 1942, Roosevelt detailed the four main areas of combat. On the Russian front, German and Soviet troops were locked in a long and bloody battle for the city of Stalingrad, in the Soviet Union. Facing a huge Soviet army, Germany sent increasingly large numbers of Nazi troops into combat and suffered heavy losses.

In the Pacific Ocean, the United States had stopped one major Japanese offensive and inflicted heavy losses on the Japanese fleet. However, Roosevelt was aware that the Japanese still had great strength. Meanwhile, Allied forces battled for control of the Mediterranean Sea and Indian Ocean. In Europe, the war's fourth arena, the main action was the offensive against Germany.

Roosevelt met often with his generals and with Allied leaders to discuss strategy. He was in particularly close contact with Winston Churchill, meeting with him nine times during the war and speaking with him often by telephone. Roosevelt and Churchill also met with Soviet dictator Joseph Stalin, though not

Roosevelt meets with Joseph Stalin (left) and Churchill (right) in November 1943. The three leaders formed an allied front, but they didn't always agree on strategy.

as often. Roosevelt worked to create a personal connection with Stalin. But Roosevelt and Stalin had little in common, making a true connection between the men difficult. Additionally, Stalin was suspicious of the meetings Roosevelt and Churchill had without him and did not trust either man.

Roosevelt had to juggle demands from Stalin and Churchill. Stalin wanted the Allies to push directly into Germany from the north, launching an attack from Britain and then crossing German-occupied France. Churchill promoted attacking the Axis forces in Italy, which he considered an easier target. Roosevelt supported Churchill's plan. The invasion of Germany could wait until the Allies had built up more momentum.

WAR REFUGEE BOARD

Throughout the 1930s, European Jews had been desperate to flee Nazi-occupied territory. Many sought asylum in the United States. In the first years of the war, the United States did not have a rescue policy for Jewish refugees and even turned some away. At first, Roosevelt was reluctant to take any action that could upset anti-immigration advocates. He and Churchill both believed that the best way to rescue European Jews was to win the war as swiftly as possible. But as news leaked out about the Nazi mass murder of Jews, some US citizens and leaders began demanding that the United States do more to help.

One of those leaders was Henry Morgenthau, Roosevelt's secretary of the treasury. On January 16, 1944, Morgenthau presented Roosevelt with evidence that the US State Department was actively sabotaging some rescue efforts. In response, Roosevelt established the War Refugee Board by executive order. It would eventually rescue about two hundred thousand Jews, although critics protested the measure was too little, too late.

TUSKEGEE AIRMEN

During World War II, the United States military was racially segregated. African Americans served in all-black units, and most were assigned to low-ranking jobs as cooks, drivers, and maintenance workers. In 1939 Roosevelt signed a law creating a special college training program that would allow black soldiers to take more advanced positions. One highly trained unit was a squadron of African American pilots known as the Tuskegee Airmen. Created by the War Department in 1941, the unit trained at the Tuskegee Air Force Base in Alabama, and they flew many successful missions as bomber escorts in Europe. In 1941 First Lady Eleanor Roosevelt visited the airmen and flew with one of the pilots, gaining press coverage and national recognition for the squadron.

Tuskegee airmen pose with a fighter plane in May 1942.

THE MANHATTAN PROJECT

The war ground on. The Allies slowly won territory, mile after bloody mile. Victory began to seem likely, but the cost of that victory was steadily rising. Each day the conflict continued, more Americans lost their lives. Roosevelt searched for a way to end the war quickly.

Albert Einstein, a German-born physicist, had written to Roosevelt in 1939, telling the president about recent experiments that could lead to a new type of extremely powerful bomb. The US military knew that the German government was already working on creating an atomic weapon. Having such an advanced weapon could give any nation a decisive upper hand in the war. So Roosevelt launched a program to develop an atomic bomb for the US military.

The program, known as the Manhattan Project, was shrouded in secrecy. Roosevelt withheld information about it even from most of his top advisers. He kept no copies of its reports in the White House files. Few of the people working on the project knew its purpose, and the scientists who did were under constant surveillance by the Federal Bureau of Investigation (FBI). Roosevelt told his secretary, Grace Tully, "I can't tell you what it is, Grace, but if it works, and pray God it does, it will save many American lives."

★ CHAPTER SEVEN ★

WINNING PEACE

By the end of 1943, the Allies were winning the war on every front. They had pushed Germany out of Africa. Italy had surrendered, its dictator Mussolini had been removed from power, and the new Italian government had joined the Allies. The German offensive against the Soviet Union faltered after the loss of more than three hundred thousand German troops. In the Pacific, Americans were advancing toward Japan. With Germany in a weakened state, Roosevelt and the other Allied leaders agreed it was time to launch a northern invasion into France and, from there, into Germany's heartland.

The Germans had heavily fortified the northern coast of Europe. Their "Atlantic Wall" stretched from Denmark

Benito Mussolini declared himself dictator of Italy in 1925. He ruled the country for nearly twenty years.

to the border between Spain and France. Anywhere the Allies chose to strike, German minefields and machine guns would be waiting. Allied commanders decided to land at Normandy on the northern coast of France. Called D-Day, the attack would take place on June 6, 1944.

Roosevelt knew that D-Day could be the tipping point of the war. The night before the invasion, he couldn't sleep. On the morning of June 6, US general Dwight D. Eisenhower led the combined Allied troops in their assault on the beaches of Normandy. Three thousand men died, but the assault was successful. The Allies had secured a beachhead in France.

Thousands of American troops wade to shore during the D-Day attack on the shores of Normandy, France, on June 6, 1944.

THE GI BILL

With victory closer than ever, Roosevelt turned his thoughts to America's transition to a peacetime economy. He had vivid memories of the Bonus Army of desperate World War I veterans. One of his priorities was to make sure that World War II's soldiers would not face the same struggles after they returned home.

In his July 28, 1943, Fireside Chat, he told the people, "Among many other things we are, today, laying plans for the return to civilian life of our gallant men and women in the armed services. They must not be [released from the military] into an environment of inflation and unemployment, to a place on a breadline, or on a corner selling apples." He outlined the programs he hoped to create.

His hopes were realized in the form of the GI Bill, developed by Harry W. Colmery, a former national commander of the American Legion and former Republican Party national chairman. Roosevelt signed the bill into law on June 22, 1944. The bill provided veterans with pensions, medical care, unemployment benefits, funding for education, and loan guarantees for those who wanted to purchase homes or start businesses.

FOURTH PRESIDENTIAL TERM

The 1944 presidential election was approaching. In visibly poor health, Roosevelt said that he didn't want to run. Yet with the war still on, he felt obliged to do so. Senator Harry Truman of Missouri reluctantly agreed to be his running mate. Initially, the campaign energized Roosevelt, but he was thin, exhausted, and suffering from dangerously high blood pressure. Dark circles hung under his eyes. His hands shook, and he had developed a persistent cough.

In his acceptance speech at the Democratic Convention in Chicago, he accepted his party's nomination and laid out his

vision: "What is the job before us in 1944? First, to win the war—to win the war fast, to win it overpoweringly. Second, to form worldwide international organizations, and to arrange to use the armed forces of the sovereign Nations of the world to make another war impossible within the foreseeable future. And third, to build an economy for our returning veterans and for all Americans—which will provide employment and provide decent standards of living."

Roosevelt won reelection with 53 percent of the popular vote. He saw this as support for his vision of America's larger role on the world stage.

Senator Harry Truman (left) of Missouri meets with Roosevelt at the White House in 1944. Truman agreed to join the Roosevelt ticket as the vice presidential candidate that same year.

YALTA CONFERENCE

Just weeks after his fourth term began, on February 4, 1945, Roosevelt flew to the Soviet resort town of Yalta to meet with his fellow Allied leaders. The meeting became known as the Yalta Conference. Though the war in the Pacific dragged on, the end was in sight for the war in Europe. Roosevelt, Churchill, and Stalin hammered out the details of the future peace. This proved difficult. Stalin didn't fully trust Roosevelt and Churchill, and they didn't fully trust him. Their countries' postwar goals were very different. Each side would have to compromise.

Churchill, Roosevelt, and Stalin meet at the Yalta Conference in Febraury 1945. The three men discussed plans to end the war.

Seeing the potential of a long fight still ahead in the Pacific, Roosevelt asked for Stalin's pledge that Russia would join the fight against Japan. In exchange, Roosevelt and Churchill agreed that the future governments of the nations bordering the Soviet Union should be "friendly" to the Soviet regime and its Communist Party. The Soviets promised that all these nations would have free elections. After the war, Germany would be divided among the winning nations.

THE COLD WAR

The wartime alliance between the Communist Soviet Union and the democratic nations of the United States and Britain was tense. The Soviet government was run by the Communist Party, which stood in direct opposition to the United States' capitalist economic system and democratic government system. Roosevelt believed that in negotiating with Stalin at Yalta, he had done the best that he could. But the Yalta Agreement would eventually lead to Communist control over Eastern Europe and to the Cold War. This conflict was not a "hot" war in which the opposing sides directly attack each other. Instead it was a decades-long standoff during which the United States and the Soviet Union competed fiercely for global political and economic power, as well as for scientific and cultural influence. The two nations extended their rivalry by becoming involved in conflicts in other nations, but they did not officially or directly battle each other. The Cold War ended with the breakup of the Soviet Union in 1991.

The three leaders also made plans for the formation of an international peacekeeping organization, which would become the United Nations. They agreed that the organization would be headed by a General Assembly made up of representatives from all member states. Major peacekeeping responsibilities would fall to the Security Council. This council would include representatives from the United States, Britain, the Soviet Union, China, and France, plus six members chosen by the permanent "Big Five" member nations. The permanent members of the Security Council would have veto power over any UN resolutions. It was Roosevelt's hope that this organization would ensure lasting global peace.

Roosevelt speaks to the press about the results of his participation in the Yalta Conference on March 1, 1945.

Upon his return from Yalta, a weary Roosevelt gave his report to Congress while seated in a wheelchair, the first time he'd ever done so. He made a joke about it, saying he'd been feeling fine until he returned home and heard all the rumors that had flown around Washington in his absence.

He told Congress that the first priority was to secure Germany's surrender as quickly as possible. Then he departed from his written speech to press the cause of the United Nations. America had a great decision to make "that will determine the fate of the United States and the world for generations to come. There can be no middle ground here. We shall have to take the responsibility for world collaboration, or we shall have to bear the responsibility for another world conflict."

CHAPTER EIGHT

LEGACY

After his post-Yalta address to Congress, Roosevelt returned to Warm Springs, Georgia, to recuperate. His cousins Laura Delano and Margaret Suckley went with him. His lover, Lucy Mercer Rutherfurd—now widowed—was also there. She and Roosevelt had corresponded in the 1920s and began meeting regularly again after her husband died in 1944. Roosevelt tried to keep his meetings with Mercer from the First Lady.

On April 12, 1945, Roosevelt was sitting for a portrait in his cottage at Warm Springs. The sixty-three-year-old president worked on a speech while the painter fussed, turning him this way and that. Roosevelt seemed very tired. They were about to break for lunch when a strange expression came over Roosevelt's face. "I have a terrific pain in the back of my head," he said. He slumped forward.

The doctor arrived ten minutes later, but it was too late. The president had suffered a massive stroke. At 3:35 p.m., Franklin Delano Roosevelt was pronounced dead.

MOURNING AT HOME

Eleanor was holding a press conference in Washington, DC, fielding questions about the United Nations, when she was called to the telephone. Laura Delano told her that Franklin had fainted. Eleanor was advised to continue with her afternoon schedule, so as not to alarm anyone, and fly to Warm Springs as soon as

Roosevelt poses for a photograph in the library at Warm Springs on the day before his death in April 1945.

she was done. Right after her next speech, Eleanor received another call. This one was from the White House press secretary, telling her to return to the White House immediately. Her hands clenched. "In my heart of hearts," she later said, "I knew what had happened, but one does not actually formulate these terrible thoughts until they are spoken."

Vice President Harry Truman was summoned to the White House at the same time. When he arrived, Eleanor told him the president was dead. Stunned, Truman asked if there was anything he could do for her. "Is there anything *we* can do for *you?*" she responded. "You are the one in trouble now."

Men and women gathered in Washington, DC, after news of Roosevelt's death on April 12, 1945.

The nation was shocked by the news of Roosevelt's death. Restaurants and theaters closed. Baseball games were canceled. The nation's four major radio networks suspended commercial broadcasting. Church bells tolled. Neighbors gathered to share their grief, weeping openly. One young soldier from a group that had gathered outside the White House explained, "I felt as if I knew him. I felt as if he knew me—and I felt as if he liked me."

WORLD REACTION

People across the world mourned the passing of a great leader. Schools and courts in Italy closed to honor the man who had helped liberate them from fascism. France observed three days of national mourning for Roosevelt. In Moscow, the Soviet Union's capital, black-bordered flags flew at half-mast and crowds gathered in the streets and subway stations. Even the prime minister of Japan offered his sympathy to the American people.

Churchill was at an uncharacteristic loss for words. Visibly upset, he asked the House of Commons, part of the British legislature, to close down out of respect for the US president. Perhaps he had spoken his feelings best a few months before, upon seeing off Roosevelt's plane after a meeting in North Africa. He told an American diplomat, "If anything happened to that man, I couldn't stand it. He is the truest friend; he has the farthest vision; he is the greatest man I have ever known."

The day after Roosevelt's death, a funeral train carrying the president's flag-draped coffin left Warm Springs, Georgia. Thousands of men, women, and children lined the route. The train stopped in Washington, DC, and a funeral service was

Mourners line the streets of Pennsylvania Avenue in Washington, DC, to watch Roosevelt's funeral procession on April 24, 1945.

conducted in the East Room of the White House. Then the train continued north to Hyde Park, where Franklin Delano Roosevelt was buried in his mother's rose garden.

WAR'S END

Two weeks after Roosevelt died, as the Allies surrounded the German capital of Berlin, Hitler killed himself. Twenty-five days later, on May 7, 1945, Germany surrendered. In August President Truman ordered the US military to drop two atomic bombs, one on the Japanese city of Hiroshima, the other on Nagasaki. The bombs completely destroyed both cities, and on August 14, 1945, Japan surrendered. World War II was over.

New Yorkers wave flags and throw paper to celebrate the news of Japan's surrender to the Allies on August 14, 1945. Families looked forward to welcoming veterans home from the war.

Nine months after Roosevelt's death, the first meeting of the United Nations General Assembly was held in London, England. Eleanor Roosevelt attended as one of the delegates, an appointment she would hold for six years.

Millions of soldiers returning from World War II took advantage of the GI Bill's educational opportunities. This eased pressure on the job market, which meant only a small percentage of veterans ended up unemployed. Many veterans also used the GI Bill's home loan benefits to buy homes of their own, once an unreachable dream for most Americans. The boom in home sales rippled through the economy, ushering in a decades-long period of prosperity.

ROOSEVELT'S LEGACY

"I dream dreams but am, at the same time, an intensely practical person," Roosevelt had written during the war. He was always willing to experiment. If one program or approach didn't work, he would try another.

His New Deal programs weren't able to completely lift the Great Depression. Unemployment had remained high in 1940, and the economy didn't fully recover until the United States began gearing up for World War II. But Roosevelt did bring the United States back from the brink of economic disaster, and he laid the foundation for future economic stability and prosperity.

He also changed Americans' expectations of their government. During his time in office, the federal government took a greater role in regulating corporations and in ensuring the well-being of its citizens. Roosevelt didn't just act as chief executive, someone who put policies into effect. He also acted as chief legislator, creating the laws and policies that he later carried out. In this way, he enlarged the role of the presidency.

UNIVERSAL DECLARATION OF HUMAN RIGHTS

In response to the atrocities of World War II, the United Nations hoped to safeguard the rights of individuals everywhere in the world. The UN General Assembly established an eighteen-person committee to draw up a document that would spell out the rights of all people, regardless of nationality, sex, religion, or other status. Eleanor Roosevelt chaired the committee and was instrumental in drawing up the United Nations Universal Declaration of Human Rights. This declaration continues to serve as a guide for international law. It says that all people are entitled to be free from slavery, torture, discrimination, and other abuses.

Eleanor Roosevelt holds a draft of the United Nations Universal Declaration of Human Rights in 1948. She was instrumental in drawing up the document.

Roosevelt's policies still affect the lives of Americans in the twenty-first century. New Deal legislation protects workers' right to organize and bargain collectively. The minimum wage, the forty-hour workweek, and overtime pay exist because of New Deal legislation. Because of the New Deal, Americans receive Social Security, which provides retirement benefits for older Americans, unemployment insurance for those who have lost their jobs, disability benefits, and benefits for orphaned children.

The GI Bill lives on, providing benefits for veterans. The FDIC still insures bank deposits. And investors are better informed because of Roosevelt's Securities and Exchange Act.

The impact of Roosevelt's programs is visible in every corner of the country. Americans drive over bridges and on the 10,000 miles (16,093 kilometers) of highway constructed under the WPA. They enjoy the parks created and the forests planted by the CCC. Farmers continue to receive payments for not planting surplus crops. The TVA still provides electricity for more than nine million customers across seven states.

When Roosevelt took office, the United States was staunchly isolationist. He led the nation through the trials of World War II to become a global power—the leader in world affairs that it is in the twenty-first century. Roosevelt was also a major architect of the United Nations, and his wife, Eleanor, continued that work, serving the organization as a delegate.

ROOSEVELT'S VISION

Franklin Delano Roosevelt was born to great money and power. Yet just as his political career was rising, polio paralyzed his legs and stalled his momentum. Roosevelt could have allowed his disability to thwart his ambition to public service. Instead, he persevered. He continued his career, struggling to achieve his

vision for a greater America. He imagined a nation that achieved economic fairness and in which government took a more active role in safeguarding the well-being of its citizens.

He also fought to promote his vision for a better world. The day he died, Roosevelt was preparing a speech, which was published after his death. Roosevelt had written, "Today we have learned in the agony of war that great power involves great responsibility." He went on, "But the mere conquest of our enemies is not enough. We must go on to do all in our power to conquer the doubts and fears, the ignorance and the greed which made this horror [World War II] possible. . . . The work my friends, is peace."

TIMELINE

1882: Franklin Delano Roosevelt is born.

1905: Roosevelt marries Anna Eleanor Roosevelt on March 17.

1910: Roosevelt is elected to the New York State Senate.

1913: Roosevelt is appointed assistant secretary of the navy by President Woodrow Wilson.

1914: World War I begins in Europe. Roosevelt urges Congress to build up the US Navy.

1917: The United States enters World War I. Roosevelt helps oversee naval operations in the war.

1918: World War I ends. Eleanor discovers Roosevelt's affair with Lucy Mercer.

1920: Roosevelt runs as vice president to the Democratic presidential candidate, James Cox. They lose to Republican Warren Harding. Roosevelt returns to private life as a lawyer.

1921: Roosevelt is stricken with polio while vacationing with his family on Campobello Island, New Brunswick, Canada.

1929–1932:   Roosevelt serves as governor of New York.

1929: The stock market crashes, setting off the Great Depression.

1933: Roosevelt is sworn in as president of the United States on March 4. During his first one hundred days, he enacts a variety of legislation to help an economy stalled by the Great Depression.

1935: The bills creating the WPA and Social Security are passed.

1936: Roosevelt is reelected for a second term as president.

1939: Germany invades Poland, starting World War II.

1940: Roosevelt is elected for a third term as president.

1941: Japan attacks Pearl Harbor, and the United States enters World War II.

1944: The GI Bill is enacted. Roosevelt is reelected for a fourth term as president.

1945: Roosevelt dies of a stroke on April 12 in Warm Springs, Georgia, at the age of sixty-three. Germany surrenders on May 8. Japan surrenders on August 14, ending World War II. The United Nations is established on October 24.

SOURCE NOTES

6   James MacGregor Burns, "*Roosevelt: The Soldier of Freedom, 1940-1945*" (New York: Harcourt Brace Jovanovich, 1970), 161, in H. W. Brands, *Traitor to His Class: The Privileged Life and Radical Presidency of Franklin Delano Roosevelt* (New York: Doubleday, 2008), 3–4.

9   Franklin D. Roosevelt, "FDR's 'Day of Infamy' Speech: Crafting a Call to Arms," *Prologue Magazine* 3, no. 4 (Winter 2001), National Archives, accessed September 16, 2014, http://www.archives.gov /publications/prologue/2001/winter/crafting-day-of-infamy -speech.html.

12   H. W. Brands, *Traitor to His Class: The Privileged Life and Radical Presidency of Franklin Delano Roosevelt* (New York: Doubleday, 2008), 30.

12   Ibid., 31.

17   "Biography: Franklin Delano Roosevelt," *American Experience,* PBS, accessed April 14, 2015, http://www.pbs.org/wgbh /americanexperience/features/biography/eleanor-Fdr /?flavour=mobile.

21   Frances Perkins, *The Roosevelt I Knew,* (New York: Viking Press, 1946), 29.

24   Franklin D. Roosevelt, "Message to the New York Legislature, August 28, 1931," in Franklin Delano Roosevelt, *Great Speeches*, ed. John Grafton, accessed June 1, 2005, https://books.google.com /books?id=31PCAgAAQBAJ&pg=PA11&lpg=PA11&dq=To+those +unfortunate+citizens,+aid+must+be+extended+by+the+gove rnment+%E2%80%93+not+as+a+matter+of+charity+but+as+a +matter+of+social+duty.&source=bl&ots=wORQ4mPftp&sig=2 IdM_yKDZxWP65a1P0oXHhwS1ig&hl=en&sa=X&ei=dlr4VM2k GMLFgwSz-4LACg&ved=0CCUQ6AEwAQ#v=onepage&q=To%20 those%20unfortunate%20citizens%2C%20aid%20must%20 be%20extended%20by%20the%20government%20%E2%80%93%20 not%20as%20a%20matter%20of%20charity%20but%20as%20a%20 matter%20of%20social%20duty.&f=false, Google Play Book.

24   "Franklin D. Roosevelt: Address Accepting the Presidential Nomination at the Convention in Chicago, July 1932," *The American Presidency Project*, accessed October 1, 2014, http://www. presidency.ucsb.edu/ws/?pid=75174.

24   "The Bonus Army," *Digital History*, accessed April 14, 2015, http://www.digitalhistory.uh.edu/disp_textbook .cfm?smtID=2&psid=3438.

24   Brands, *Traitor to His Class*, 268.

26   James MacGregor Burns, *Roosevelt: The Lion and the Fox* (New York: Harcourt Brace Jovanovich, 1956), 163.

27   Franklin D. Roosevelt, "On the Bank Crisis," First Fireside Chat, March 12, 1933, Franklin D. Roosevelt Presidential Library and Museum, accessed November 3, 2014, http://docs.Fdrlibrary .marist.edu/031233.html.

28   "Fireside Chats," *History*, accessed October, 24, 2014. http://www .history.com/topics/fireside-chats

29   Roosevelt, "On the Bank Crisis."

31   Ibid.

34   Perkins, *The Roosevelt I Knew*, 76.

37   Franklin D. Roosevelt, "Roosevelt congratulates the million and a half workers of the Civilian Conservation Corps." April 17, 1936, *American Experience, PBS*, accessed May 12, 2015. http://www.pbs .org/wgbh/americanexperience/features/primary-resources/fdr -anniversary/?flavour=mobile

41   Franklin D. Roosevelt, "Message to Congress Suggesting the Tennessee Valley Authority," April 10, 1933, *Franklin D. Roosevelt Presidential Library and Museum*, accessed November 3, 2014, http://docs.fdrlibrary.marist.edu/odtvacon.html.

42–43   Franklin D. Roosevelt, "Presidential Statement Signing the Social Security Act—August 14, 1935," *Social Security Administration*, accessed March 10, 2015, http://www.ssa.gov/history/fdrsignstate .html.

43   Perkins, *The Roosevelt I Knew*, 70.

44   Brands, *Traitor to His Class*, 325.

45   Franklin D. Roosevelt, "Address on Agricultural Adjustment Act, 1935," *American Experience*, PBS, accessed October 7, 2014, http://www.pbs.org/wgbh/americanexperience/features/primary-resources/Fdr-aaa/.

48   Franklin D. Roosevelt, "Address to the Chamber of Congress on the Recovery Program," May 4, 1933, *The American Presidency Project*, accessed November 3, 2014, http://www.presidency.ucsb.edu/ws/?pid=14634.

49–50   "FDR and the Wagner Act," *Franklin D. Roosevelt Presidential Library and Museum*, accessed March 5, 2015, http://www.fdrlibrary.marist.edu/aboutfdr/wagneract.html.

52   Franklin D. Roosevelt, "Campaign Address, October 14, 1936," *Teaching American History*, accessed October 8, 2014, http://teachingamericanhistory.org/library/document/campaign-address/.

54   Benito Mussolini, "What Is Fascism, 1932," *Modern History Sourcebook*, Fordham University, accessed October 9, 2014, http://www.fordham.edu/halsall/mod/mussolini-fascism.asp.

55   Brands, *Traitor to His Class*, 481.

56   Ibid., 483.

57   Ibid., 510.

58   Franklin D. Roosevelt, "Fireside Chat, September 3, 1939," *The American Presidency Project*, accessed March 6, 2015, http://www.presidency.ucsb.edu/ws/?pid=15801.

60   Susan Dunn, *1940: FDR, Willkie, Lindbergh, Hitler—the Election Amid the Storm* (New Haven, CT: Yale University Press, 2013), 184.

61   Franklin D. Roosevelt, "Fireside Chat, December 29, 1940," *The American Presidency Project*, accessed October 10, 2014, http://www.presidency.ucsb.edu/ws/?pid=15917.

62   Franklin D. Roosevelt, "The Four Freedoms Speech, Delivered 6 January 1941," *American Rhetoric,* Top 100 Speeches, accessed October 13, 2014, http://www.americanrhetoric.com/speeches/fdrthefourfreedoms.htm

65   Brands, *Traitor to His Class*, 658.

66   Carl J. Schneider and Dorothy Schneider, *World War II* (New York: Facts on File, 2003), 256.

67   Franklin D. Roosevelt, "Annual Budget Message, January 5, 1952," *The American Presidency Project*, accessed October 14, 2014, http://www.presidency.ucsb.edu/ws/?pid=16231.

73   James MacGregor Burns, *Roosevelt: The Soldier of Freedom 1940-1945* (New York: Harcourt Brace Jovanovich, 1970), 456.

76   Franklin D. Roosevelt, "On Progress of War and Plans for Peace," Fireside Chat, July 28, 1943, *Franklin D. Roosevelt Presidential Library and Museum*, accessed November 17, 2014, http://docs.Fdrlibrary.marist.edu/072843.html.

77   Franklin D. Roosevelt, "Address to the Democratic National Convention in Chicago, July 20, 1944," *The American Presidency Project*, accessed October 15, 2014, http://www.presidency.ucsb.edu/ws/?pid=16537.

81   Brands, *Traitor to His Class*, 807–808.

82   Ibid., 812.

83   Ibid., 816.

83   Ibid.

84   Perkins, *The Roosevelt I Knew*, 6.

85   Brands, *Traitor to His Class*, 824.

87   Burns, *Roosevelt: The Soldier of Freedom*, 609.

90   Franklin D. Roosevelt, "Undelivered Address Prepared for Jefferson Day," April 13, 1945, *The American Presidency Project*, accessed October 17, 2014, http://www.presidency.ucsb.edu/ws/?pid=16602.

GLOSSARY

Allied forces: a coalition whose major members were Great Britain, France, the Soviet Union, the United States, and China, which fought against the Axis powers in World War II

Axis powers: a partnership whose principal members were Germany, Italy, and Japan, which fought against the Allied forces in World War II

Black Thursday: Thursday, October 24, 1929, when the stock market plunged, leading to the Wall Street crash and the Great Depression

Bonus Army: tens of thousands of World War I veterans and their families who camped out in Washington, DC, during the depths of the Great Depression, demanding that the government pay them their promised bonuses early

capitalism: an economic system based on private ownership of businesses

D-Day: June 6, 1944, when the Allies invaded the fortified coast of Normandy, France, to begin a sweep across Europe to the heartland of Nazi Germany during World War II

embargo: a ban on trade with a specific country

fascism: an authoritarian system of government, ruled by a dictator

Fireside Chats: a series of thirty informal radio broadcasts that Roosevelt gave between 1933 and 1944 to directly address American citizens

free enterprise: competition among businesses with little government control

gold standard: a promise by participating countries to set the value of their currency at a specified amount of gold. The currency can at any time be converted to gold.

Great Depression: an economic downturn that began in the United States in 1929 and eventually spread around the globe. It was the worst economic depression ever experienced in the industrial world and caused financial panic, a decline in production, and high unemployment.

isolationist: a person who believes that a country should not become involved in the affairs of other nations

Kristallnacht: a series of attacks on the Jewish populations of German and German-occupied territories on November 9 and 10, 1938. This event is also called the night of broken glass in reference to the many broken windows of ransacked Jewish homes and businesses.

League of Nations: an organization established after World War I to provide a forum for settling international disputes. It was initially proposed by President Woodrow Wilson, but the United States never joined.

mortgage: a legal agreement in which a person borrows money to buy property, such as a house, and pays back the money over a period of years

Nazi: a member of the German Nazi Party. The party's policies included state control of the economy, racist nationalism, and national expansion. Adolf Hitler was the leader of the Nazi Party from 1921 until his death in 1945.

sovereignty: the right to self-rule and independence, without outside interference

vocational training: training for a specific career or trade

SELECTED BIBLIOGRAPHY

Brands, H. W. *Traitor to His Class: The Privileged Life and Radical Presidency of Franklin Delano Roosevelt*. New York, Doubleday, 2008.

"Biography of Franklin D. Roosevelt." *Franklin D. Roosevelt Presidential Library and Museum*. Accessed April 14, 2015. http://www.fdrlibrary.marist.edu.

Burns, James MacGregor. *Roosevelt: The Lion and the Fox*. New York: Harcourt Brace Jovanovich, 1956.

———. *Roosevelt: The Soldier of Freedom, 1940–1945*. New York: Harcourt Brace Jovanovich, 1970.

"Franklin D. Roosevelt: Impact and Legacy." *Miller Center, University of Virginia*. Accessed April 14, 2015. http://millercenter.org/president /biography/fdroosevelt-impact-and-legacy.

"Franklin Delano Roosevelt." *United States Holocaust Memorial Museum*. Accessed April 14, 2015. http://www.ushmm.org/wlc/en/article .php?ModuleId=10007411.

"Kristallnacht: A Nation-wide Pogrom, November 9-10, 1938." *United States Holocaust Memorial Museum*. Accessed April 14. 2015. http://www.ushmm .org/wlc/en/article.php?ModuleId=10005201.

"Neutrality Acts, 1930s." *US Department of State, Office of the Historian*. Accessed April 14, 2015. https://history.state.gov/milestones/1921-1936 /neutrality-acts.

Perkins, Frances. *The Roosevelt I Knew*. New York: Viking, 1946.

"Public Papers of the Presidents." *The American Presidency Project*. Accessed April 14, 2015. http://www.presidency.ucsb.edu/ws.

Schlesinger, Arthur M., Jr. *The Age of Roosevelt: The Politics of Upheaval*. Boston: Houghton Mifflin, 1960.

"The Yalta Conference, 1945." *US Department of State, Office of the Historian*. Accessed April 14, 2015. https://history.state.gov/milestones/1937-1945 /yalta-conf.

FURTHER INFORMATION

Bolden, Tonya. *Roosevelt's Alphabet Soup: New Deal America, 1932–1939*. New York: Alfred A. Knopf, 2010.
Find out what life was like during the Great Depression and how Roosevelt's programs affected Americans then and in the twenty-first century.

"Classroom": *The Roosevelts—An Intimate History*
http://www.pbs.org/kenburns/the-roosevelts/classroom.
Find out more about Theodore, Eleanor, and Franklin Roosevelt at this companion site from PBS for the popular Ken Burns series on the Roosevelts.

Coetzee, Frans, and Marilyn Shevin Coetzee. *The World in Flames: A World War II Sourcebook*. New York: Oxford University Press, 2011.
Read more about World War II in the words of those who lived through it.

"For Students": Franklin D. Roosevelt Presidential Library and Museum
http://www.fdrlibrary.marist.edu/education/students.html
This site is a great source of photographs and fast and fun facts about Franklin Roosevelt.

The Great Depression for Students: Library of Congress
http://www.loc.gov/teachers/classroommaterials/themes/great-depression/students.html
View multimedia American Treasure exhibits on the Great Depression.

Kesselring, Mari. *How to Analyze the Works of Franklin D. Roosevelt*. Minneapolis: Abdo, 2013.
Franklin D. Roosevelt was a media master. Discover what made his speeches work so well.

Lindop, Edmund, with Margaret J. Goldstein. *America in the 1930s*. Minneapolis: Twenty-First Century Books, 2010.
Learn more about American culture, politics, and economics during the 1930s, from dancing the swing to the birth of King Kong.

———. *America in the 1940s*. Minneapolis: Twenty-First Century Books, 2010.
From the baseball star Joe DiMaggio to the crooner Frank Sinatra, find out more about life in the 1940s.

Morris-Lipsman, Arlene. *Presidential Races: Campaigning for the White House.* Minneapolis: Twenty-First Century Books, 2012.
Find out how campaigning has changed from the days of George Washington to Barack Obama.

Roosevelt, Eleanor. *Autobiography of Eleanor Roosevelt.* New York: Harper Perennial, 2014.
Read, in her own words, the story of Eleanor's momentous life as a crusader for human rights, a participant in world events, and one of America's first delegates to the United Nations.

"See You Next Year—High School Yearbooks from WWII": The National WWII Museum
http://www.ww2yearbooks.org/home
See the events of World War II through the eyes of teens who lived through it.

INDEX

PHOTO ACKNOWLEDGMENTS

The images in this book are used with the permission of: Franklin D. Roosevelt Presidential Library, pp. 1, 2 (handwriting), 11, 12, 13 (right), 16, 17, 21, 25, 30, 37, 39, 40, 46, 51, 70, 83; © iStockphoto.com/Nic_Taylor (backgrounds); © iStockphoto.com/hudiemm (backgrounds); Library of Congress LC-USZ62-120408, p. 2; © iStockphoto.com/WilshireImages, p. 3 (bunting); © Independent Picture Service, p. 3 (signature); National Archives (080-G-19948), p. 7; National Archives (208-CN-3992), p. 8; Library of Congress (LC-DIG-ppmsca-36063), p. 13 (left); National Archives (196960), p. 14; © Bettmann/CORBIS, p. 18; National Archives (306-NT-163-554C), p. 23; Library of Congress (LC-DIG-hec-46853), p. 26; National Archives (6728517), p. 28; © Bettmann/CORBIS, p. 33; © Photo by New York Times Co./Getty Images, p. 34; National Archives (196155), p. 38; Library of Congress (LC-DIG-hec-38273), p. 42; Library of Congress (LC-DIG-fsa-8b32410), p. 45; National Archives, p. 47; © Bettmann/CORBIS, p. 49; Library of Congress (LC-DIG-hec-47244), p. 53; © United States Holocaust Memorial Museum, p. 55; © United States Holocaust Memorial Museum, courtesy of Trudy Isenberg, p. 57; © Lt. L C Priest/ IWM/Getty Images, p. 59; © Bettmann/CORBIS, p. 61; National Archives (538660), p. 65; National Archives (208-AA-352QQ-5), p. 68; © Wikimedia Commons, p. 72; © Roger Viollet/Getty Images, p. 74; National Archives (111-SC-320902), p. 75; National Archives (66-2610), p. 77; National Archives (111-SC-260486), p. 78; © George Skadding/The LIFE Picture Collection/Getty Images, p. 80; National Archives (520710), p. 84; Library of Congress (LC-USZ62-67439), p. 85; National Archives (208-N-43468), p. 86; National Archives (24427-2011-001), p. 88.

Front cover: Franklin D. Roosevelt Presidential Library (portrait and handwriting); © Independent Picture Service (signature); © iStockphoto.com/WilshireImages (flag bunting).

Back cover: © iStockphoto.com/hudiemm (sunburst); © iStockphoto.com/Nic_Taylor (parchment).

ABOUT THE AUTHOR

Linda Crotta Brennan is the award-winning author of more than twenty
books for children, including *When Rivers Burned: The Earth Story*, *The Black
Regiment of the American Revolution*, *Flannel Kisses*, and *Marshmallow Kisses*.
After earning a master's degree in education, Ms. Brennan taught for
many years and worked as the Teen Program Coordinator at the Coventry
Public Library. She now writes full-time, her golden retriever at her feet,
surrounded by her husband, grown daughters, and grandchildren.